MASTER THIS!

Golf

Clive Gifford

WAYLAND

Northamptonshire Libraries
& Information Service
60 000 009 243
Peters 28-Sep-2009
C796.35 £12.99

First published in 2009 by Wayland

Copyright © Wayland 2009

Hachette Children's Books
338 Euston Road
London NW1 3BH

Wayland Australia
Level 17/207 Kent Street
Sydney NSW 2000

All rights reserved.

Senior editor: Claire Shanahan
Produced by Tall Tree Ltd
Editor, Tall Tree: Jon Richards
Designer: Ed Simkins

British Library Cataloguing in Publication Data
Gifford, Clive.
Golf. -- (Master this)
1. Golf--Juvenile literature.
I. Title II. Series
796.3'523-dc22

ISBN: 9780750258319

Printed in China

Wayland is a division of Hachette Children's Books, an Hachette UK company.

www.hachette.co.uk

Picture credits

All photographs taken by Michael Wicks, except:
t-top, b-bottom, l-left, r-right, c-centre
cover Dreamstime.com/Photogolfer, 5 Dreamstime.com/Photogolfer, 6c Dreamstime.com/Vincent Giordano, 6b Dreamstime.com/Lai Leng Yiap, 7cr istockphoto.com/Kati Molin, 7bl istockphoto.com/Chen Chun Wu, 7bc istockphoto.com/Matthew Porter, 7br Dreamstime.com/Alex Melnick, 8bl Dreamstime.com/Miltudog, 10 Dreamstime.com/Nip, 11br Dreamstime.com/James Phelps, 21bl Dreamstime.com/Photogolfer, 27bl Jason A. DeMott /Icon SMI/Corbis, 29 Dreamstime.com/Brandon Tucker

The website addresses (URLs) included in this book were valid at the time of going to press. However, because of the nature of the Internet, it is possible that some addresses may have changed, or sites may have changed or closed down since publication. While the author and publisher regret any inconvenience this may cause the readers, no responsibility for any such changes can be accepted by either the author or the publisher.

Disclaimer

In preparation of this book, all due care has been exercised with regard to the advice, activities and techniques depicted. The publishers regret that they can accept no liability for any loss or injury sustained. When learning a new sport it is important to get expert tuition and to follow a manufacturer's instructions.

Acknowledgements

The publishers would like to thank Harpenden Golf Club (www.harpendengolfclub.co.uk), Peter Lane PGA Advanced Professional, Elliot Bourke, Ollie Drain and Spencer Morton for their help with this book.

Contents

The game of golf

A golfer uses clubs to strike a golf ball, trying to take as few shots as possible to hit the ball into a small hole. A full game, or **round**, of golf is usually played over 18 holes.

History

Games similar to golf can be traced back to a number of ancient civilisations, including the ancient Chinese and Romans. The game grew in importance in Scotland in the 18th and 19th centuries, from where it was exported around the world. Today, there are four major tournaments for men: the Masters, the US Open and the PGA (Professional Golfers' Association) Championship held in the United States of America (USA), and the Open held in the United Kingdom (UK).

Skill and power

Golf may look like a gentle game but it calls for incredible skill, power, nerve and concentration. Top players can hit a ball more than 300 metres (328 yards), and they can also hit a delicate shot from just 100 metres (109 yards) away to within centimetres of the hole. Golfers need mental strength to handle the pressure of a tough shot and to allow for weather conditions and hazards.

Hitting the ball into the hole requires concentration and, when a golfer is successful, it can be really satisfying.

Lorena Ochoa is one of the world's most successful women golfers. She won her first national golf tournament at the age of seven. At the other end of the scale, Elsie Mclean managed to hit a hole in one at the age of 102.

Golf for all

Golf is a game played by male and female players of all ages. You do not need to be tall or athletic to play golf, but you do need a good level of fitness to play well. A round of golf involves walking 6–9 kilometres, and the fitter you are, the less tired you will be when taking shots near the end of the game. For a beginner, a full round of golf can involve making 120 shots or more and may last four hours. It is important to have eaten healthily beforehand, around one-and-a-half to two hours before playing. Players should carry a bottle of water with them on the course, to avoid becoming dehydrated during a game.

Top tip

Carry a healthy snack bar and a drink in your golf bag to give you an energy boost during a game. Fresh fruit, especially an apple or banana, is a good source of energy during a long round of golf.

Clubs and balls

Golf clubs are available for left- or right-handed players (the clubs shown here are for right-handed players). Players use a variety of clubs, called **irons, woods, wedges** and **putters.** A golfer is allowed to carry up to 14 different clubs.

Top tip

Take good care of your golf clubs. Keep them somewhere dry. Clean all the heads using soapy water and an old toothbrush to get dirt from out of the grooves on the club face.

Around a club

At the top of a club is a rubber grip, which stops the club from slipping in your hands. At the other end of the club is the club face. The face is the part that makes contact with the ball during a shot. The shaft is in the middle of the club. Its length varies with different types of club. Woods and long irons have long shafts. This means that the head on these clubs travels faster during the swing, hitting the ball harder.

Golf club shafts come in various lengths to suit players of different height. If you are buying a set of clubs, you should take advice from a golf professional or the shop owner about which length of shaft would best suit you.

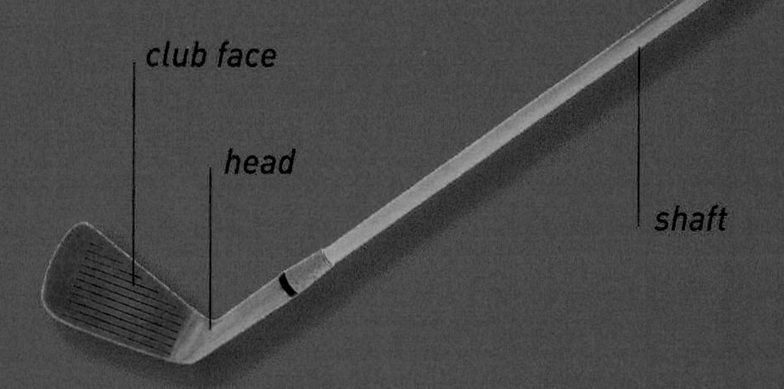

Golf balls

A golf ball must measure at least 4.3 centimetres wide. The surface is covered with small indents, called dimples. These help the ball to fly through the air, making it travel farther.

Degrees of loft

The **loft** of a club is the angle between the club face and the shaft. The greater this angle, the higher the ball will fly and the shorter the distance it will travel. Typically, a driver (for hitting long distances) will have an angle of 10 degrees, while a sand wedge's loft angle might be 58 degrees.

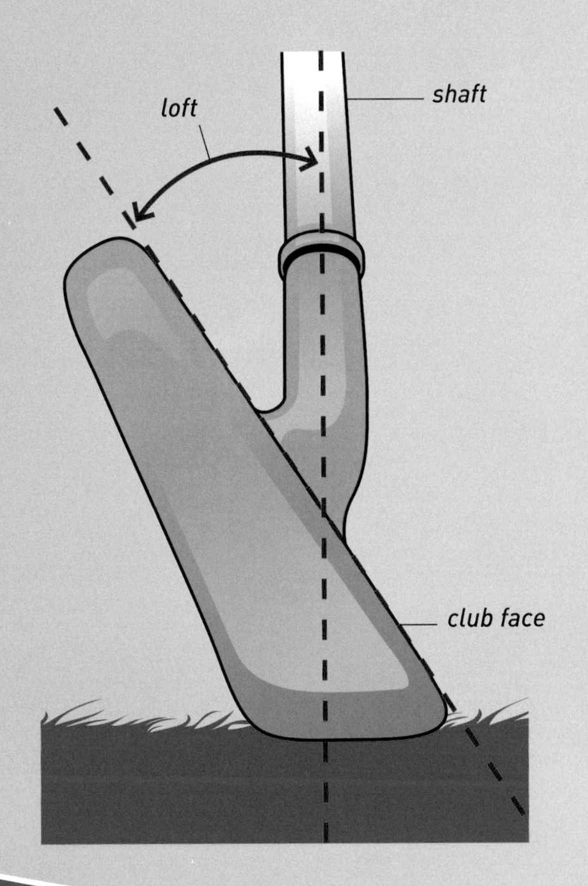

When the golf club hits the ball, the bottom edge of the club face makes contact under the ball. This lifts the ball and pushes it forwards as the club swings through.

Types of club

Clubs can be divided into three main groups – irons, woods and putters. Each type of club is designed for shots in different conditions or on different parts of a hole (see page 10). Irons are used to hit various distances from the **tee area**, **fairway** or **rough**. Woods are used to hit long distances off the tee or fairway. The putter is for shots on the **green**.

IRONS
Irons are numbered from one to nine. The higher the number, the greater the loft and the less distance the ball will travel. A two iron can hit a ball up to 180 metres (197 yards) while a nine iron can hit a ball about 120 metres (131 yards).

WEDGES
*Wedges are a special type of iron, and are used to hit onto the green from short distances or to get out of a **bunker**.*

WOODS
Woods have large heads and are designed to hit farther than irons. A driver is a special type of wood that can be used to hit the ball 230 metres (251 yards).

PUTTER
Putters are designed to hit the ball along the ground. They are used on the green or from the edge of the green.

Clothing and kit

Golf is played in most kinds of weather, so players have to be prepared for all conditions. Different golf courses have different rules about what can be worn, so you should check before you play.

Head to toe

Golf clothing usually consists of a short-sleeved shirt, trousers or skirt, and a jumper. The clothing should not be so tight that it restricts your movement, but it should also not be so baggy that it gets in the way during a shot. You should always pack clothing and equipment for bad weather. A large umbrella is essential, as are a hat and a waterproof jacket and trousers.

Star file

ELDRICK 'TIGER' WOODS
World number one

Tiger Woods was playing golf on television at the age of two and winning junior tournaments by the age of eight. In 1997, he secured his first major title at the age of just 22. Tiger Woods has been the world number-one ranked golfer for more than 500 weeks since 1997, even though he took many months off through injury in 2008.

*Golfers need to dress appropriately for the weather, with a sweater for mild, dry days. This golfer is carrying his golf bag, but he could also use a **trolley**.*

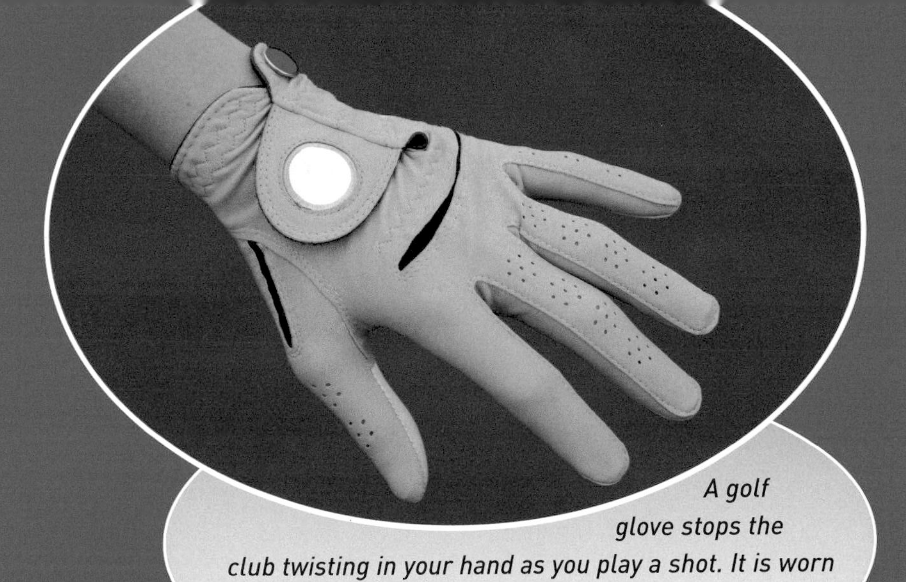

A golf glove stops the club twisting in your hand as you play a shot. It is worn on the left hand for a right-handed player and on the right for a left-hander.

Shoes and bag

Golf shoes have small rubber pimples or short spikes on their soles for more grip in wetter weather. As a round of golf involves a lot of walking, your shoes need to fit well and be comfortable. A golfer's bag not only carries the clubs, but it also has pockets for carrying extra equipment, such as spare balls, golf tees (see page 18) and a **pitch repairer**.

This golfer is wearing wet-weather clothing, which is lightweight and loose. Other wet-weather equipment includes a small towel to dry your clubs' grips.

Pitch repair

This ball has left a dent, or pitch mark, on the green.

A pitch repairer allows you to fix the dent. Push the fork of the pitch repairer in and around the dent.

Then push the fork under the dent and lift up the grass. Finally, flatten the area gently using your putter or shoe.

Places to play

Golf courses are made up of nine or 18 holes. Many courses also have facilities, such as a driving range and a practice green, where you can work on different shots.

Top tip

At the driving range, do not get into the habit of just hitting as many balls as quickly as possible. Think about each shot and set yourself a target, but most of all, take your time.

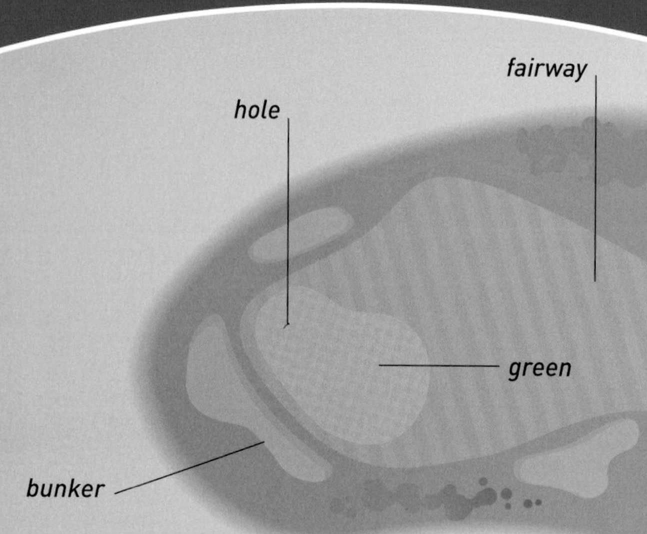

Around a hole

Golf holes vary in length from around 100 metres (109 yards) to more than 500 metres (547 yards). In the UK and the USA, golf holes are measured in yards, but they are measured in metres in Europe. The first shot, or **drive**, is played from the tee area (see pages 18–19). A path of short grass, called the fairway, leads away from the tee area. On either side are areas of longer grass, called rough, and usually trees. At the end of the fairway is the green, which surrounds the hole. The hole itself is marked by a flag. Each hole may have a number of hazards, such as bunkers, streams and lakes.

A golfer practises his iron and wood shots at a driving range (left) and his putting at a practice green (below). These places allow golfers to develop their technique by playing shots over and over again, without having to walk long distances between shots, as they do during a game of golf.

Driving, pitching and putting

A driving range consists of a series of bays in which golfers swing at balls placed on mats. Buckets of balls are bought and are hit using whatever club golfers wish to practise with. A driving range has marked target greens or distance flags so you can see how far each shot travels. **Pitch and putt** courses are fun places to practise shorter shots and putting. Each hole is quite short – usually 40–90 metres (44–98 yards) long – yet they still provide the challenge of getting the ball as near to the flag as possible. Practice greens are also good places to improve your putting stroke by repeatedly putting balls into the holes.

Star file

PADRAIG HARRINGTON
Irish master

Irishman Padraig Harrington studied to become an accountant, but at the age of 24 he became a professional golfer and joined the European Tour in 1996. A popular and successful member of the tour with 14 tournament wins, Harrington's game went up a level in 2007 and 2008, when he won three Majors (the Open twice and the PGA Championship). He looks set to win several more in the future.

Playing a round

Playing on a full course for the first time can be a little nerve-wracking. Each of the 18 holes will have been designed to present the golfer with different challenges.

Playing etiquette

Golfers are expected to be honest. For example, if a golfer nudges their ball with a club, then another shot should be added to their score. Players should also be fair and show respect for other golfers and the course. This is known as **etiquette**. It includes never playing a shot until the way ahead is clear, never delaying play and always caring for the golf course.

Raking the sand

After playing a shot from the bunker, this player rakes the sand smooth for the next golfers to play the hole. He walks backwards as he rakes, making sure that he smooths over the footsteps he left when walking into the bunker.

As one golfer plays a shot, his partners stand to one side. They stay still and silent while watching the shot so that they can follow the ball. If the ball flies towards other golfers, they will shout, 'Fore!' as a warning.

Waving through

This player waves through a group of golfers behind him. Golfers should wave through the following group if they are playing slowly or if they are having trouble finding a ball.

Up to par

Each hole on a golf course has a par score. This is the number of shots in which a good golfer will complete the hole – so a par-four hole should be completed in four shots. Completing a hole in one more shot than par is known as a bogey, and two more shots is a double bogey. One shot less than par is called a birdie, two shots less than par is an eagle and three shots below par is called an albatross.

It is good golfing etiquette to 'tend the flag' for another player's putt if they are on the green. The golfer on the left is tending the flag, holding it until the ball rolls towards the hole, when he will lift out the flag.

These players have just completed a hole. While one of them replaces the flag in the hole, the others walk off the green as quickly as possible, leaving it clear for the next group of players. Players should also leave their bags by the side of the green, so they do not damage it.

Grip and stance

How you hold the club is called your grip. The way you position yourself and the club before starting your swing is known as **addressing** the ball. These two elements are important for a good shot.

Top tip

There are a number of different grips you can use to hold a club, including the interlocking grip, shown below for a right-handed player. A golf coach will show you which grip suits you best.

Gripping stuff

Your hands are the only parts of your body that come into contact with the club. This is why getting a good grip is so important. A good grip may feel odd at first, but you should practise it whenever you can. Over time, it will become second nature so that you know immediately how to hold the club.

Interlocking grip

1

Place your left hand around the grip. The knuckle of the left thumb should be in line with your left arm.

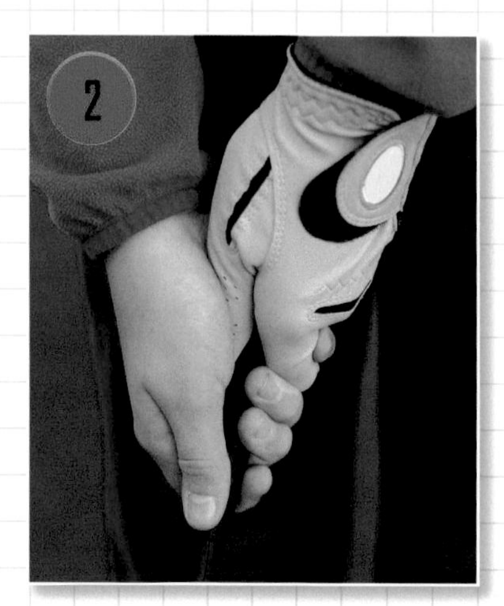

2

Wrap your right hand below your left. The right thumb knuckle should be in line with the right arm.

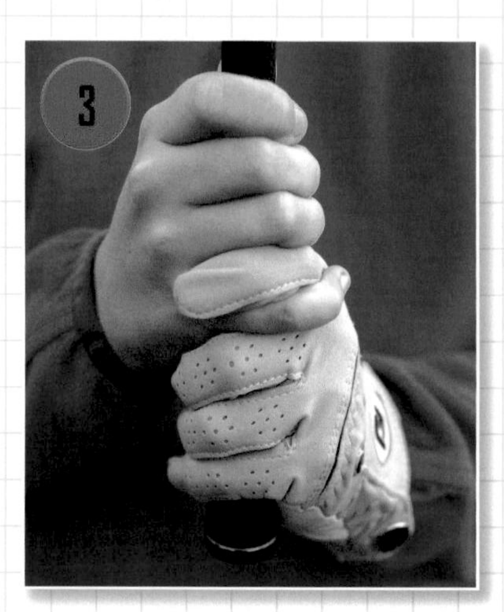

3

The index finger of your left hand and the little finger of your right should interlock with each other.

Addressing the ball

Addressing the ball starts with you lining up your shot. Taking up the correct stance when addressing the ball may seem unusual at first, but given practice, it should feel comfortable and balanced. A golf coach can show you how far you should stand away from the ball. A simple rule to follow is to place the bottom, or sole, of the club level on the ground, to see the angle at which the club shaft sticks out.

right shoulder slightly lower than the left, as the right hand grips lower down the club

eyes on the ball but chin up enough so that head can turn easily

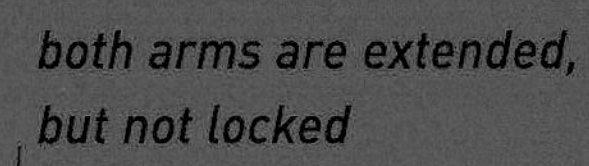

both arms are extended, but not locked

arms hang down in front

hands are held in line with the ball

olfer leans forwards with weight over front part of his feet

knees are flexed

When addressing the ball, it is important to stay relaxed. Any tensing of the muscles will affect your shot.

Feet position

When lining up your feet, think about train tracks. One track should run in a line through your two feet, while another track should run from the ball to the target. This player is using two clubs on the ground to help line up his 'tracks'.

Swinging

An accurate golf swing can result in the ball travelling a long distance. The swing can be broken down into three parts: **backswing, downswing** and **follow through**. These are put together in one flowing movement.

The backswing

The backswing starts with the club taken back and away from the ball with a sweeping movement. The movement starts from the shoulders, which turn, followed by the arms, then the body. As the body turns, your weight moves more onto your back leg. Your left leg bends slightly to the right, but without causing you to lose balance.

This golfer has reached the top of his backswing. Pressure on his left thumb from the club has 'cocked' his wrists to form an 'L' shape with his arm.

The swing

This player moves his weight onto his back foot while taking the golf club back on the backswing.

At the top of the backswing, the golfer's hands and arms form an 'L' shape and his knees stay relaxed.

Common faults

There are many reasons for poor shots. Some are caused by a loss of balance from a poor stance or because your backswing and downswing are too fast. Keep the club head under control at all times and do not try to force the club. Try also to keep your knees bent throughout the swing. Rising as you swing down or lifting your head causes many players to hit only the top of the ball or to miss it altogether.

Downswing and follow through

The backswing coils your body like a spring. The downswing is the uncoiling action that creates the power of the shot. After hitting the ball, the swing continues and is now on its follow through. The player does not lift their head up but, instead, swivels it around. The hips turn, weight transfers to the front foot and the swing ends with the player's chest and head facing the target. The club should end up over the back of the left shoulder for a right-handed golfer.

During the downswing, the player keeps his arms together to sweep the club through the ball.

After hitting the ball, the player keeps his head down during the follow through.

With his weight transferred onto his front foot, the player completes the follow through.

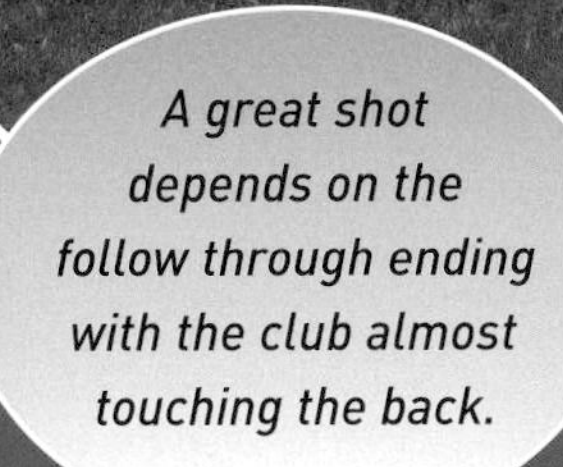

A great shot depends on the follow through ending with the club almost touching the back.

Driving

Every hole begins on the tee area with the drive – the first shot. A good drive can set you up well for the rest of the hole. If the hole is a par three, then you may be able to reach the green with your drive.

Top tip

When driving, do not just aim for a general part of the fairway. Pick a small target in the distance beyond the green, such as a tree. This will help you focus on lining up your drive accurately.

Tee areas

Most golf courses have different tee areas for men, women and junior golfers. These are all indicated with colour-coded tee markers. Choose a smooth piece of the tee without divots (pieces of earth) near your feet or the ball. On shorter holes, always wait until players ahead have left the green. On longer holes, make sure all players ahead are well out of your range before playing your shot.

This ball has been placed on a tee before a drive. A tee is a T-shaped piece of plastic or wood on which the ball rests. The tee lifts the ball off the ground, making it easier to hit. Tees can be used only for the first shot on a hole.

Tee markers

On the tee area, coloured pairs of tee markers indicate where different players should start. For example, on some courses male players should tee off between the yellow markers and junior players from between the blue.

Shot selection

Practising at a driving range will teach you how far you can hit the ball with each club. By studying the hole ahead, golfers can pick out places on the fairway they can reach with a shot.

Sometimes, golfers may have to play a shorter drive than their maximum because of hazards on the hole, such as a bunker. This is known as laying up. At all times, a golfer's choice of drive should be about leaving the ball in the best possible position for their second shot.

This player has driven off from behind a pair of tee markers. His feet are shoulder width apart and his swing is smooth and relaxed.

Spotting hazards

Before playing your first shot, study the hole ahead to spot any hazards. Below are some of the things to look out for. If there are a lot of hazards on one side of the fairway, play your drive from that side of the tee area. This will help you to hit away from trouble.

trees
bushes and shrubs
rough
bunker
fairway
green
bunker
bunker

Fairway shots

Many golf shots are played from the fairway. These are often played with an iron, although certain woods can be used.

Fairway play

After the drive, the player farthest from the flag plays the next shot. Golfers are allowed to take practice swings before making the shot. A good iron shot from the fairway, especially on soft ground, often takes a divot with it. Always collect and carefully replace the divot after your shot.

Divots

Once the divot is replaced, press it down gently into place with your shoe. Do not stamp down on it hard as this may destroy the grass roots.

This golfer is about to play a fairway shot with a five iron. He is aiming to make clean, accurate contact with the ball to send it straight towards the green.

Decisions, decisions

Each shot from the fairway needs careful thought to work out where to send the ball. Experienced golfers also take into account the wind and course conditions. A dry course will see the ball run on much further than a soggy wet course. Golfers will also look at where the ball is lying and its relation to where they stand when playing the shot.

Playing below

This golfer is playing a shot with his ball lying lower than his feet. With his weight over his heels, he holds the club at the top of the grip. He may choose to use a three-quarter swing to have more control over the shot.

Star file

VIJAY SINGH
Pacific hero

The Pacific Ocean's most successful golfer, Vijay Singh is renowned for practising longer and harder than many of his rivals. It has paid dividends as the Fijian has won the Masters and the PGA Championship twice. He was the world's number-one golfer for 32 weeks in 2004 and 2005 and is rarely out of the top five in the world rankings.

Up and downhill

On an upward slope, the golfer sets his hips in line with the slope. He chooses a club with a lower loft angle because the slope will lift his shot.

On a downward slope, he sets his hips in line with the slope. He chooses a club with a higher loft angle because his shot will be lower.

The short game

Shorter shots, usually aiming for the green, are known as a golfer's short game. These include high-option shots, which fly high, and low-option shots, which fly lower and bounce farther. A good short game can cut many shots from your score.

Playing it high

High-flying shots are played with short irons – nine iron, pitching wedge or sand wedge. They are great shots for clearing an obstacle such as a bunker in front of a green. Hit well, high-option shots tend to generate **backspin** on the ball, and this can stop the ball running on past the target.

High-option

This golfer's ball is lying below the green with a small hump in front of him.

With his weight spread over both feet, the golfer draws his club back.

Swinging the club through the ball, he keeps his head down and does not lean back.

He follows through to guide the ball over the hump and towards the target.

Keeping it low

Low-option shots are used when faced with a relatively flat green ahead and no obstacles between the ball and the flag. They are played with a seven iron and the ball travels much lower than a high-option shot. The ball bounces on or just short of the green and rolls on.

When playing a low-option shot, golfers should keep their wrists firm and not cock them back as they do with most other shots.

Low-option

With no obstacle between the ball and the hole, this golfer can play a low-option shot.

His backswing is short, with the club shaft roughly parallel to the ground.

His wrists are firm during the shot so that the club head does not travel too quickly.

The ball flies lower, bounces sooner but rolls farther than a high-option shot.

Getting out of trouble

All golfers find their balls in trouble on some holes during a round. Players need to know the rules about these situations and how to play the ball out of danger.

The rough on either side of the fairway presents great challenges to players. This longer grass makes it harder to play a shot as the grass can catch the club head and twist it.

As it lies

A golf ball is meant to always be played where it stops, or 'as it lies'. If you find your ball in the rough or in a divot hole in the fairway, that is just tough luck. If your ball is not in a hazard, you are allowed to remove loose bits and pieces, such as leaves and twigs, near the ball, providing you do not move it. If your ball lands in an area of ground marked as 'ground under repair', you must not play it from there. Instead, you can take a free drop without adding a shot to your score.

Going sideways

This golfer's ball has landed right behind some bushes. He cannot play towards the hole and has to play out sideways. In some cases, you may have to play away from the hole to get out of trouble.

Drops

If you think your ball is unplayable, such as right up against a tree, you can take a drop. You add a shot to your score and drop the ball two club lengths away from where it lies. A drop is made from arm's length and shoulder height – you cannot just place the ball on the ground.

Bunkers

When playing a shot from a bunker, the head of the golf club cannot touch the sand when addressing the ball. Instead, the club head has to be raised slightly before taking the shot.

Dropping

This player's ball has an unplayable lie behind a tree. He measures out two club lengths away from where the ball stopped.

The player drops the ball at this point, making sure this is no nearer to the hole. He will take his shot from this position.

Bunker play

This golfer is playing a shot from a bunker next to a green. With his feet nestled in the sand, he takes his club back.

Keeping his knees bent, he takes a full swing and aims to bring his club down into the sand 7–8 centimetres behind the ball.

With a firm grip on the club throughout the shot, he brings the club through the ball and follows through to keep the ball on target.

Putting

In a typical round of golf, putting can make up around half of the shots played. It makes sense to work hard on this part of your game to avoid taking three or four putts on each hole and ruining your score.

Top tip

When reading a green, try to look at your putt from both behind the ball and from the far side of the hole. If a playing partner putts first, watch their shot, noting how the ball moves.

Putting strategy

Judging how hard to hit the ball in order for it to travel the right distance is the most important thing on longer putts. With shorter putts, getting the line right to send the ball into the hole is crucial. In all cases, aim to leave yourself with as short a second putt as possible. To control the distance of a putt, players vary how far they pull the club back on the backswing rather than change the speed of their swing.

This player is crouching to read the green, looking for any slopes. The condition of the green is important, too. A putt on a dry green, for example, will travel faster and farther than a putt on a wet green.

Marking the ball

If your ball needs a clean or is in the way of another player's putt, you can remove it by marking the ball. You place a marker behind the ball, without nudging it, and then pick up the ball.

Putting strokes

The club head on a putter has little or no loft angle (see page 7), so it rolls the ball along the ground rather than lifting it. Compared to a full swing, the putting stroke is short and extremely simple, but care must be taken to get everything precise and correct.

Stand so that your eyes are directly over the ball. The putter is positioned behind the ball and facing in the direction you want to send the ball. The swing should be smooth and relaxed, and like the swing of a pendulum. Your wrists should be kept firm, without them bending at any point during the stroke.

Star file

YANI TSENG
Rising star

Tseng started playing golf when she was six, and for three years was Taiwan's best amateur female golfer. She was still a teenager when she turned professional in 2007 and joined the Ladies Professional Golf Association (LPGA) tour the following year. Her debut season started well with her becoming the youngest ever winner of the LPGA Championship and coming second in the British Open. She ended 2008 as the world number-three ranked female golfer.

On the green

At the start of the stroke, the player takes the club back slowly, keeping it low to the ground.

Keeping the club speed constant, the club head brushes the top of the grass as it hits the ball.

The player keeps his head down while the putter face follows through. This helps to send the ball in the right direction.

Taking it further

There are many ways to take golf further, from helping out at your local golf club to entering a junior competition. The best junior golfers may go on to represent regional or national teams as amateurs or they may even turn professional.

Top tip

Try to watch as many golf competitions as you can, either on television or live at a golf course. Study how professionals play and you will pick up some important tips.

Getting on course

Many golf courses are for members only. Membership can be expensive and clubs can be difficult to join. However, some courses offer special deals for young players. Alternatively, there are many public golf courses around that often offer a reduced fee for junior players. Some young golfers look to fund playing the game by becoming caddies. They carry the bags of adult golfers around a course.

The very best way to improve your game is to have lessons with an experienced professional. They can spot errors in your stance and swing and suggest solutions and useful tips.

Scoring for matches

When playing in a match, golfers can score their game in a variety of ways. Strokeplay, for example, compares the number of shots each player takes to complete the game, and the player who records the fewest shots is the winner.

In matchplay scoring, golfers play against each other to win a hole by completing it in the fewest shots. Golfers are awarded a point for each hole they win. If the hole is drawn, then each golfer receives half a point. Matchplay scoring is usually used during team competitions, while strokeplay is used for individual matches.

The handicap system

The handicap system allows amateur golfers of different abilities to play in competitions against each other. A handicap is effectively a number of shots (usually between one and 36), which are removed from their final score in a game to give players their net score. The better the golfer, the lower the handicap will be. So if a player with a handicap of 13, completes a game in 84 strokes, their net score is 71. The net score will be the same as another player, with a handicap of 8, who completed the game in just 79 shots.

Professional competitions are usually for individual golfers. However, there are some team events, such as the Ryder Cup for men's teams from the USA and Europe. Here, the USA team celebrates winning in 2008.

Glossary

addressing when a golfer stands next to the ball just before playing a shot.
backspin when the ball spins in the opposite direction from the way it is travelling. Backspin can make a ball stop quickly after pitching or roll back once it has landed.
backswing the part of the golf swing where the club is taken back and away from the ball.
bunker a pit filled with sand that is found along the fairway and around the green.
downswing the part of the golf swing where the club is brought down towards the ball.
drive the first shot on a golf hole which is made from the tee area.
etiquette how a person should behave. This includes looking after the golf course and making sure that other players are out of range of your shots.
fairway a wide path of short grass leading up to the green.
flexed keeping something bent and supple.
follow through the part of the golf swing after the ball has made contact, where the club is pulled around until it is over the left shoulder of a right-handed player.
green an area of very short grass that surrounds the hole.
irons a type of golf club that is used for shots from the tee area, along the fairway and to get out of hazards.
loft angle the angle between the face of the club and the shaft. A club with a higher loft angle will send the ball higher.
pitch and putt a type of golf course with shorter holes than a normal course.
pitch repairer a pronged tool used to remove pitch marks from the green.
putters a type of golf club that has no loft angle and is used on the green to roll the ball towards the hole.
rough areas of long grass that are found on either side of the fairway.
round a game of golf, usually consisting of 18 holes.
tee area the area at the start of a hole from where the first shot is played.
trolley a small, two-wheeled cart designed to carry a golf bag and clubs.
wedges a type of golf club with a high loft angle used to get out of hazards and for high shots near the green.
woods a type of golf club with a large rounded head used for shots from the tee area and sometimes from the fairway.

Golfing organisations

There are several organisations and associations around the world that are involved in running the game of golf. These range from international bodies to small, regional groups.

The Professional Golfers' Association (PGA) has several bodies around the world, organising competitions for men's golf.

The women's equivalent of the PGA is the Ladies Professional Golf Association (LPGA), which has organisations in several countries around the world.

In the UK, the English Golf Union oversees the sport for amateur players. It looks after the interests of 1,900 golf courses and has nearly 740,000 members.

Further reading

There are plenty of books available for the newcomer as well as the more experienced golfer.

Inside Sport: Golf Clive Gifford (Wayland, 2009)
Know Your Sport: Golf Clive Gifford (Franklin Watts, 2008)
Teach Yourself: Golf David Davies and Patricia Davies (Hodder Education, 2006)

Websites

The Internet is a great place for information on techniques, advice, explanations of the key rules and videos of different skills.

www.rookiegolf.com
A website for junior golfers that includes a section on making a career out of golf.

www.younggolfer.co.uk
A useful website with explanations of golf terms, etiquette and rules, as well as lots of tips to improve how you play.

www.juniorlinks.com
A great website packed with information on golf rules, coaching tips and equipment guides.

Index